Farmer's Market

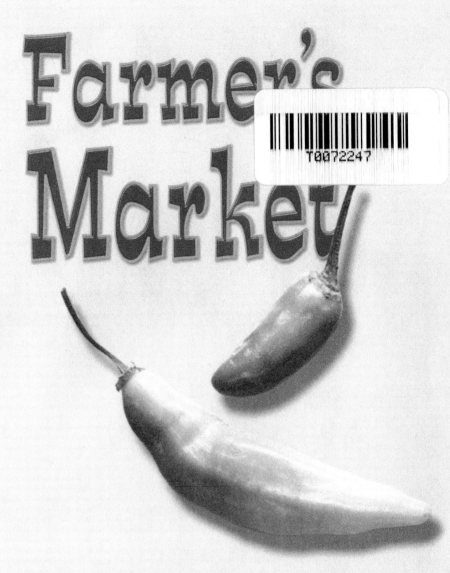

by Juan Quintana

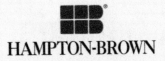

HAMPTON-BROWN

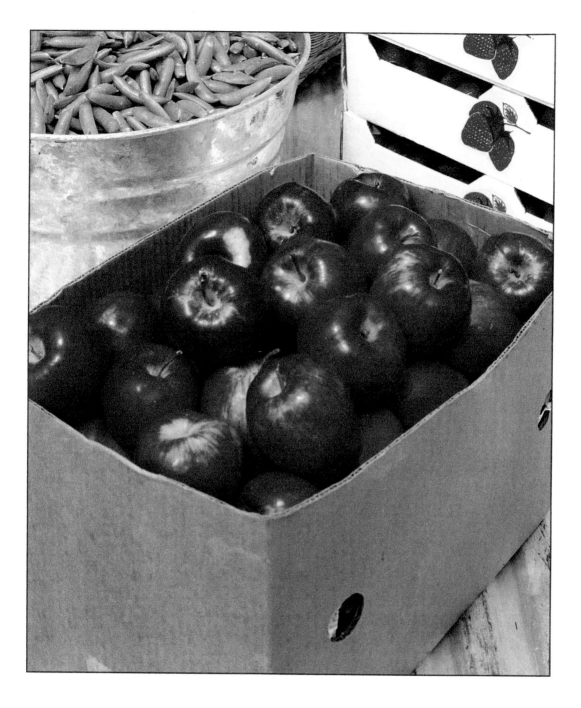

Take the apples
off the truck.

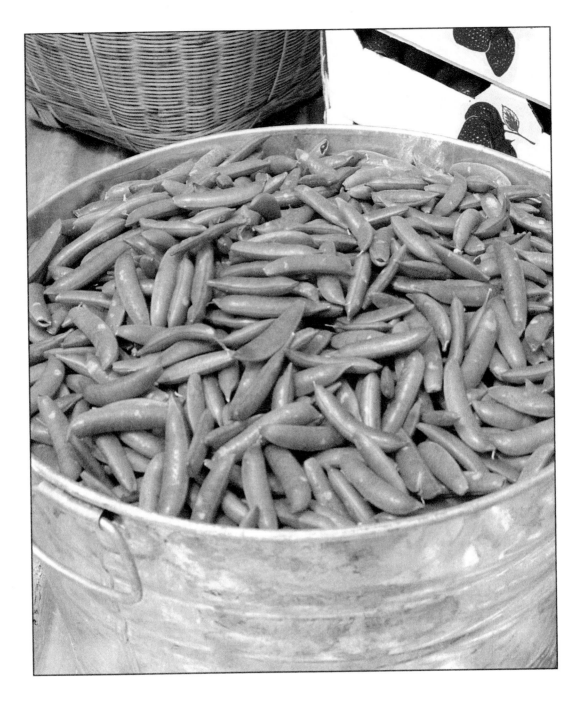

Take the peas
off the truck.

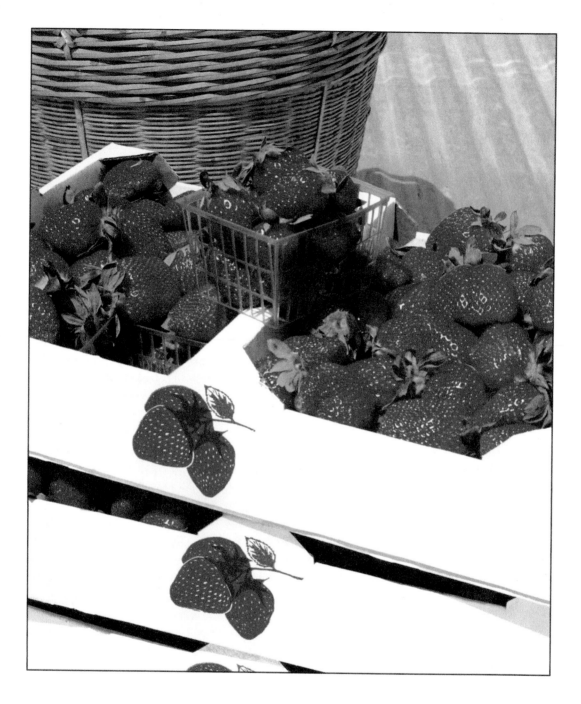

Take the berries
off the truck.

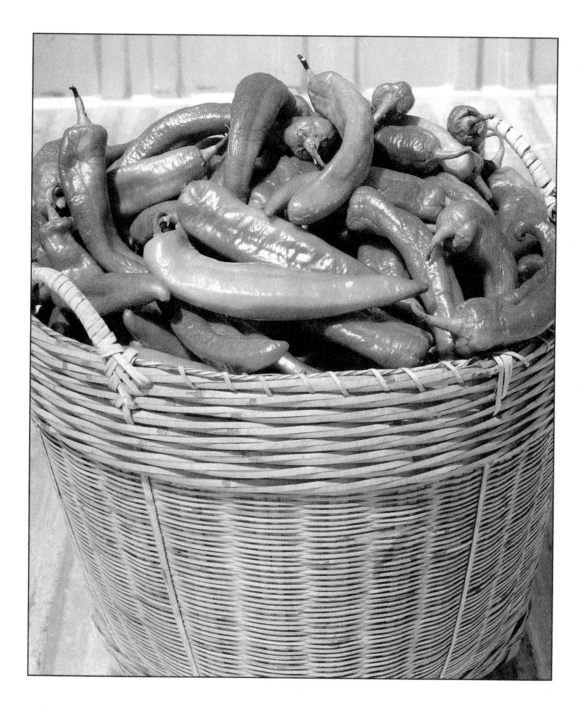

Take the chiles
off the truck.

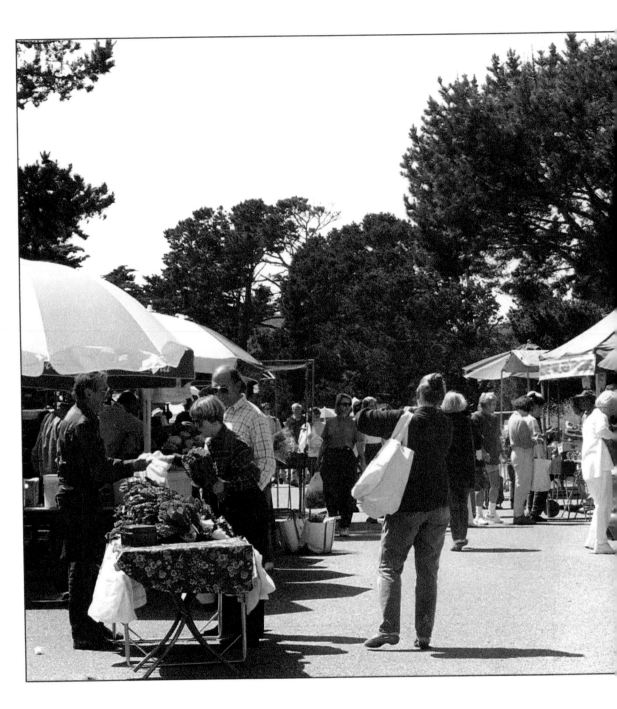

A lot of people come.

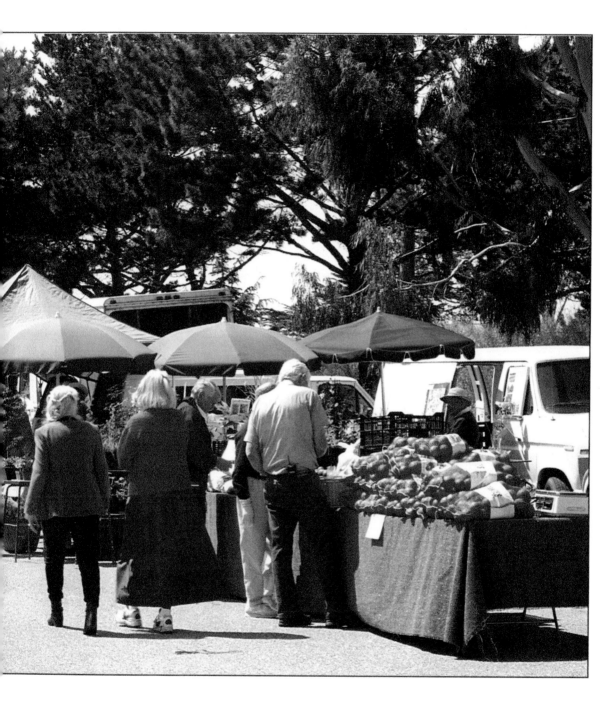

A lot of people shop.

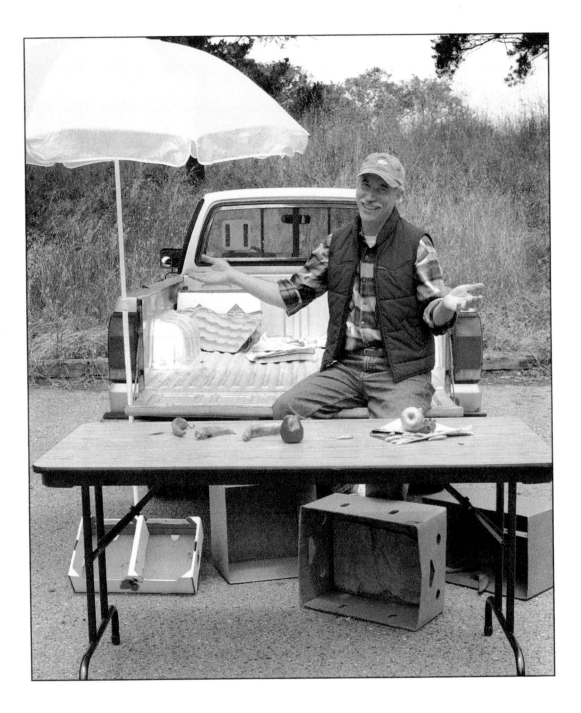

Good job, Farmer Bob!